RELATIONSHIPS
—JESUS STYLE

Also available in the Pioneer *Perspectives* series:

Prophecy in the Church	Martin Scott
Radical Evangelism	Pete Gilbert
The Role and Ministry of Women	Martin Scott

For further information on the Pioneer *Perspectives* series and Pioneer, please write to:

P.O. Box 79c, Esher, Surrey, KT10 9LP

RELATIONSHIPS —JESUS STYLE

Stuart Lindsell

WORD PUBLISHING

Word (UK) Ltd
Milton Keynes, England

WORD AUSTRALIA
Kilsyth, Victoria, Australia

WORD COMMUNICATIONS LTD
Vancouver, B.C., Canada

STRUIK CHRISTIAN BOOKS (PTY) LTD
Maitland, South Africa

ALBY COMMERCIAL ENTERPRISES PTE LTD
Balmoral Road, Singapore

CHRISTIAN MARKETING NEW ZEALAND LTD
Havelock North, New Zealand

JENSCO LTD
Hong Kong

SALVATION BOOK CENTRE
Malaysia

RELATIONSHIPS—JESUS STYLE

© Pioneer 1992.

Published by Word (UK) Ltd. / Pioneer 1992.

ISBN 0-85009-727-4 (Australia ISBN 1-86258-211-4)

Unless otherwise indicated, Scripture quotations are from the HOLY BIBLE, NEW INTERNATIONAL VERSION (NIV). Copyright © 1973, 1978, 1984 by International Bible Society.

Other quotations are taken from the New King James Version (NKJV), copyright © 1985 by Thomas Nelson, Inc., and from the King James Version (KJV).

Front cover illustration: *Christ and the Canaanite Woman*, Rembrandt, courtesy of Bridgeman Art Library.

Reproduced, printed and bound in Great Britain for Word (UK) Ltd. by Clays Ltd., St Ives plc.

92 93 94 95 / 10 9 8 7 6 5 4 3 2 1

FOREWORD

Pioneer *Perspectives* are perhaps more than their title suggests!

They are carefully researched presentations of material, on important issues, appealing to thinking churches, creative leaders and responsible Christians.

Each *Perspective* pioneers in as much as it is at the cutting edge of biblical and theological issues. Each will continue to pioneer with new ideas, concepts and data drawn from Scripture, history and a contemporary understanding of both.

They are perspectives in as much as they aim to be an important contribution to the ongoing debate on issues such as women in ministry and leadership; prophets and prophecy in the church; biblical models of evangelism; integrating and discipling new believers; growing and building local churches and further perspectives on Christ's second coming.

Importantly, these studies use a journal style of presentation, and are written by people who are currently working out the implications of the issues they are writing about, in local churches. This is vital if we are to escape the dangerous fantasy of abstract theology without practical experience. They are not written to contribute to the paralysis of analysis—rather to feed, strengthen, nurture and inform so that we can be equipped to get God's will done, by networking the nations with the Gospel using all the resources that are available to us.

God's Word is always an event. How much we thank Him that He has left us an orderly account of what He wants us to believe, how He wants us to live, and what He wants us to do in order to bring heaven to the earth. As we embrace a better understanding of Scripture, rooted in local church, national and international mission, we shall become a part of the great eschatological purpose of bringing back the King—not for a church defeated, cowering and retiring but for one which, despite colossal odds, pressures and persecutions, is faithful to her Lord and His word. To do that we must 'search the Scriptures' to see if many of these 'new things' are true. I commend these *Perspectives* to you as they are published on a regular basis throughout these coming years.

Gerald Coates
Director Pioneer Trust/Team Leader

Pioneer consists of a team and network of churches, committed to dynamic and effective biblical Christianity.

The national team act as advisers and consultants to churches, which in many cases develop into a partnership with the Pioneer team. These are the churches keen to identify with the theology, philosophy, ethos and purpose of Pioneer. The team have a vigorous youth ministry, church-planting strategy and evangelistic emphasis.

Training courses include Equipped to Lead, Emerging Leaders and the highly successful TIE teams (Training In Evangelism).

Pioneer have also been instrumental in initiating and funding March for Jesus (with Ichthus/YWAM); Jubilee Campaign (for the suffering church worldwide); and ACET (Aids Care Education Training).

ACKNOWLEDGEMENTS

With thanks to all my friends in Pioneer People who have modelled the truth over so many years. Your faithfulness, loyalty and appreciation have contributed to my life in countless ways. I also want to thank my colleagues Martin Scott, Nigel Day and Steve Clifford for all the encouragement they have given me. Special thanks as well to my wife Jayne who both made comments on the manuscript and helped convince me that the book really was worth writing. Thank you David and Andrew for giving me some space in order to meet a fast-approaching deadline.

Finally I must acknowledge the influence of Mike Blount who gave me such a clear understanding of the importance of relationships, and Gerald Coates whose confidence in me has been a source of continuing strength.

Stuart Lindsell
May 1992

CONTENTS

CONTENTS

INTRODUCTION

The Bible is an amazingly practical book. When we read through its pages we can be in little doubt as to how God wants us to live. Far from being full of abstract doctrine, it teaches us the way in which we can experience and live life to the full. The heart of its message is not only that we can enjoy a relationship with God, but it also shows us how we can live in friendship with one another. John even says that if we claim to love God but hate our fellow believer we are liars! (1 John 4:20). If we live in a right relationship with God then we are expected to live in right relationship with one another.

For many of us however, it is in the area of relationships that we feel most inadequate. We do not find it too difficult to relate to God but our relationships with others often prove full of difficulties. They may even go badly wrong. If we develop friendships that are largely superficial then we can avoid the problems, but friendships that go deeper inevitably bring a challenge. Our immaturities, fears, sins and insecurities can often come flooding to the surface. When relationships do go wrong we often do not know why they have gone wrong or how to go about putting them right.

This book is therefore intended to focus on *a word of instruction* (1 Cor. 14:26) that Jesus gave to His disciples about their relationships together. He spoke some very practical words that the apostles later developed in the New Testament letters. The book is addressed to believers and all who are committed to the lifestyle set out for us by Jesus Himself. Just as Paul could encourage Timothy to be an example (1 Tim. 4:12), so Jesus by His words, His lifestyle, His faith in His church and purity in His relationships is our great example.

Jesus, interestingly enough, only spoke of His church on two occasions and they are both recorded for us in Matthew's gospel. The first occasion is found in Matthew 16:13–20 when Jesus and His disciples were together in Caesarea Philippi. He asked His disciples who others thought that He was and then who *they* thought He was. Simon Peter, always the first to respond, blurted out that Jesus was the Messiah, the Son of the living God. Jesus confirmed that He was correct, but added that Peter did not arrive at that conclusion by any natural deduction but received it by revelation from His Father. In other words Peter's spiritual eyes were opened by a miracle. He saw Jesus, not just as a fascinating man but as He really was—the Son of the living God.

Jesus then went on to teach that His church would be built on that fundamental revelation as to who He was. His church would be made up of all who have had their eyes opened. It would be built on the solid foundation that Jesus is God's Son. Even the gates of death and Hades itself, Jesus said, would not be able to hold back His victorious church as the message of Jesus the Messiah broke out into all the world.

The second occasion when Jesus spoke of His church is found in Matthew 18:15–20. It is this instruction to His disciples that forms the substance of this book.

> "If your brother sins against you, go and show him his fault, just between the two

of you. If he listens to you, you have won your brother over. But if he will not listen, take one or two others along, so that 'every matter may be established by the testimony of two or three witnesses.' If he refuses to listen to them, *tell it to the church*; and if he refuses to listen even to the church, treat him as you would a pagan or a tax collector. (my italics)

"I tell you the truth, whatever you bind on earth will be bound in heaven, and whatever you loose on earth will be loosed in heaven.

"Again, I tell you that if two of you on earth agree about anything you ask for, it will be done for you by my Father in heaven. For where two or three come together in my name, there I am with them."

Here Jesus clearly indicated that relationship together is at the very heart of church. Faithfulness in our relationships is the mark of God's people. These faithful relationships are so powerful that where even two or three are in agreement together, heaven is on their side.

Revelation and relationship together are therefore two fundamental foundations on which the church of Jesus is built. That incidentally is why both apostolic and prophetic ministry are essential to church foundations. Apostles build people together in relationship and prophets bring revelation (1 Cor. 3:10,11; Eph. 2:20). However, in this book we want to look at our relationships together and how we can respond to the style of relationship that Jesus has set before us.

The last words that Jesus ever gave to His

disciples were that they should teach all nations to obey *everything* that He had commanded them (Matt. 28:20). That is why we cannot pick and choose from the teaching of Jesus. We are to obey *everything* He taught.

Before we look in detail at Jesus' teaching it is important that we understand something of what it means to be a part of His church. We will look at this in the first chapter.

CHAPTER 1

THE CHURCH—GOD'S ENVIRONMENT FOR GROWTH

Proverbs 4:22 tells us that God's words are life to those who find them and health to our whole body. God undoubtedly wants His body, the church, healthy. Paul reminds us in Ephesians 5:30 that 'we are members of his body' and therefore Christ cares for us and has our well-being at heart. He has a vested interest in making sure that His body is well looked after. After all, He only has one body and we are, together, that body. It is through His body that God gets His will done in the world in which we live. That is the way He has chosen to work—through us. It is therefore important to God and His purposes in the world that He has a healthy body. However, to have a healthy body means that our relationships together have to be healthy. Our relationships together will stay healthy as we continue to pay attention to God's words.

The church is, in a sense, the environment which God has given us in which our relationships can grow. Many of us have come into the church like tender plants which need the safe environment of the greenhouse. It is not that we escape the world through living in an artificial environment— on the contrary, we are called to live in the world and love the world. The church is the genuine environment where we can be strengthened to live in a world where God's ways have been abandoned.

If we are going to grow up strong we need to understand that the world and the church are two contradictory and very different environments. The world is the place where relationships have probably caused us damage and hurt, but the church is the place where we should find healing, forgiveness, restoration and strengthening. The world puts a low value on faithfulness and commitment in relationships but the church of Jesus places a high value on them. In fact, there should be no safer and more wonderful environment to live in than the church. That environment means at least four fundamental things—acceptance, encouragement, openness and honesty, and love.

1. Acceptance

In Romans 15:7 Paul encourages the church to accept one another just as Christ has accepted us, in order to bring praise to God. Do you remember the first time you had that wonderful experience of knowing that God had accepted, forgiven and received you into His family? It is a tremendous relief and joy to know that God has not rejected us but has accepted us. We cannot understand why He should love us like He does but we know that it is true because He has accepted us. His acceptance of us underlines His great love for us. Without that fundamental knowledge and awareness of being accepted by God, our relationship with Him is unlikely to grow. After all, who wants to develop a relationship with someone who has doubts about us? God has no illusions about us—after all, it was while we were still sinners that Christ died for us. Nevertheless He accepts as we are, as someone once said, 'warts, pimples and all'.

Relationships grow and are strengthened through knowing that we are accepted. That means we do not have to try and prove ourselves or try and gain acceptance. We can relax and enjoy the relationship. We need to know that we are accepted, not just by God but also by His people. We should never feel more accepted than when we are with the church. Colour, race, gender, status, educational background, job, wealth or poverty, physical appearance, achievements or lack of achievements, are all irrelevant in God's society. What counts, Paul says, is the fact that we are a new creation (Gal. 6:15). We no longer regard one another from a worldly point of view (2 Cor. 5:16).

This means that the church is not the environment in which we have to perform well in order to be accepted. We do not have to put on special religious behaviour, wear certain clothes, dress in a certain way or adopt a certain culture. Acceptance cannot be conditional upon conformity to regulations that are not rooted in Scripture. Paul called such false standards 'human commands and teachings' (Col. 2:22).

It is amazing how quickly such arbitrary standards and legalistic expectations can creep into the church. It took me a number of years to realise that, in the particular church in which I grew up, there were certain expectations of those attending meetings. One of them was that while people were waiting for the service to start, any talking had to be in hushed tones. This was supposedly because God was present and quietness was a sign of reverence. Those who were not aware of this unwritten rule were generally made to feel unspiritual, uncomfortable and unacceptable.

The new churches are not exempt from such unwritten codes of acceptable behaviour in church. Where dancing, for example, has become an acceptable expression of worship, it is interesting how certain styles of dancing are acceptable but others are not. Obviously, not every form of dance is appropriate and anything that is sensual or sexually suggestive is clearly wrong. However, at a recent meeting of Christians where the young people began to express their love and enthusiasm for the Lord by 'moshing', a number of older Christians had difficulty accepting these young people. 'Bopping' was all right but 'moshing' was not.

Christians can also be very quick to judge one another by outward appearance, forgetting that God only looks upon the heart. A foreign visitor to a church in Surrey was shocked to see that one of the men leading the worship was wearing an earring. Another man had his hair styled with a pony tail. The denomination the visitor came from taught that such outward appearance could only mean one thing—they were homosexuals! The visitor from overseas had real difficulty accepting them as Christians. In the culture the visitor came from homosexuals identified themselves by such styles. The reaction was therefore understandable, but if we are going to be churches at the cutting edge of evangelism we cannot allow such judgements to come into our thinking.

God is the great 'heart knower'; He even shocked Peter by actually giving the Holy Spirit to the Gentiles! (Acts 15:8). God does not look at the externals of a person's life. He wants to see what is in the heart. Churches that are regularly seeing people coming to know Christ for the first time will see people manifesting all sorts of non-conformist behaviour. What the new believer will be wanting to know is, 'I know God has accepted me but will God's people?' Sadly many come to the conclusion that they will not. Statistics from mass evangelistic crusades demonstrate the point that of the thousands who come to Christ, only 47% are still attending church two years later.[1] The biblical principle is that we cannot reject those whom God has accepted. Accepting one another means that we show the same grace to others that Christ has shown to us. This attitude has to be foundational.

In the church we also have the freedom to fail. We are not an exclusive society of the successful. Jesus accepts failures. In fact someone has suggested He *only* accepts failures. He allows us to make mistakes because He knows that our mistakes do not have to make us. Jesus died for those who knew they had failed. Paul says that Christ died for us while we were still sinners (Rom. 5:8). That means He did not ask us to change before He accepted us.

In the same way we are not looking for perfection in one another. We are not demanding that others change in order to be more acceptable to us, nor to be more acceptable to God. What we *are* expecting of one another is that we grow in grace, but it is only the kindness and grace of God that causes us to change (Rom. 2:4). An evangelist once said, 'Whilst God loves us as we are, He also loves us too much to leave us as we are.' It is God's love and faithfulness that causes us to change. When people are touched by the love and grace of Jesus they begin to grow like Him. Legalism will not change any of us, but we are being changed by the Holy Spirit into the likeness of Jesus (2 Cor. 3:18).

It is a comfort to know that this change is the process of a lifetime. The Bible calls it being made holy (Heb. 10:14) and theologians call it the process of sanctification. God does not demand that we change overnight. Being aware of this, a new Christian wrote, 'Be patient with me—God hasn't finished with me yet.' Knowing that God accepts us and that we are accepted by others is the environment in which holiness blossoms.

2. Encouragement

We all need encouragement, including leaders. Encouragement is a great motivator. It builds us up (1 Thess. 5:11), bringing strength and comfort. It helps us to keep going even when things are tough. When we feel like giving up or pressures are causing us to waver in our devotion to Jesus, there is nothing like a good dose of encouragement to revitalise our energy. A speaker once described Christians as leaking buckets. Even when they are full of encouragement it eventually leaks out. 'God', the speaker said, 'has called us to be bucket fillers.' That is why we have a responsibility to be continually filling one another up. The Hebrew writer even says we should do it daily (Heb. 3:13).

It is because encouragement is so important to healthy relationships that our enemy, Satan, is a great discourager. One of his tactics is to focus on the negative and never the positive. Life is full of things that encourage as well as things that discourage, but Satan makes sure that we get them out of proportion. None of us can live under a constant sense of disapproval and discouragement. Cynicism and negativism characterise the age in which we live. It has been said that the cynic 'knows the price of everything but the value of nothing'.

We therefore need to help one another by identifying the good and positive in one another's lives. Writing to the Christians at Philippi, Paul encouraged them to concentrate on values that mattered; the admirable, the excellent, the noble, the praiseworthy. When we recognise these qualities in others we are doing what the Bible calls 'honouring one another' (Rom. 12:10).

It is always important to see ourselves as God sees us. He is full of appreciation and encouragement. When Jesus first saw Simon, He renamed him Peter—'the rock man' (John 1:42). He did not see him as he was: impulsive, volatile, unreliable, but what he would become: a rock, a solid pillar in the early church (Gal. 2:9). In the same way we need to be positively affirming one another in our worth. We are called to be looking out not for one another's failures, but for one another's strong points. The emphasis needs to be on our strengths, not our weaknesses. Encouragement always reinforces our strengths but never highlights our weaknesses. That is why prophecy is so important in the church because it is encouraging, strengthening and comforting (1 Cor. 14:3). We all need encouragement.

3. Openness and honesty

Satan works in the dark but we are called to live as children of the light (Eph. 5:8). Satan likes hidden things because he knows that secret things often conceal guilt and shame. It was Gerald Coates, the leader of the Pioneer Team, who first suggested that it is in the unshared areas of our lives that Jesus is not Lord.[2] When secret and undisclosed areas of our lives are brought into the open with one or two close friends, cleansing and often release from fear can follow. The fear of exposure can be one the devil's most effective weapons against the saints. It can be an enormous relief to know that there are one or two close friends who know all about our sins and weaknesses but still love us.

Where Jesus is Lord the power of the secret areas of our lives is broken. In fact John tells us that if we walk in light as God is in the light, then we can enjoy fellowship with one another (1 John 1:7). Just as God has not held back in revealing Himself to us, we must not hold back in making ourselves known to one another. Walking in the light simply means openness and honesty. We do not try and hide our feelings or hurts, our opinions or worries or even our sins. We bring them into the light, sharing our thoughts, confessing our sins and receiving healing in doing so (James 5:16).

Being open and honest means that we speak truth in love to one another (Eph. 4:15). The disciples of Jesus noticed that He was full of grace and truth (John 1:14). He cared enough and was gracious enough to be honest even when the truth may have hurt. To be honest requires commitment and faithfulness. If we are faithful and committed to those we love, we will not fail also to be truthful.

Openness and honesty also means that at times we will be called to admonish one another (Rom. 15:14 KJV). To admonish, according to the dictionary, is 'to correct in a friendly manner'. Our friendship together will mean helping one another to see where we need to adjust our attitudes or behaviour. If we fail to admonish then our relationships are going to be affected. Satan is always looking for an opportunity to divide us, and by walking in honesty and openness we are refusing to give him an occasion to do so.

4. Love

In Romans 15:7 we noticed that we are to accept one another *just as Christ accepted us*. In Ephesians 5:2 Paul also encourages us to 'live a life of love, *just as Christ loved us*' (my italics). Jesus is again used by Paul as the pattern for our lifestyle. Living a life of love means following Jesus' example.

Firstly, it means *unconditional love*. Jesus loved people regardless of their response. It was not conditional upon their response to Him. He loved because He was LOVE and could be no other. God shows no favouritism (Rom. 2:11); Jesus loved the last, the lost and the least. He healed ten lepers but only one came back and said thanks. He forgave those who crucified Him. He identified with prostitutes and publicans. Someone once asked a speaker what would happen if a person deliberately turned their back on God's love. The answer came: 'In which case God's love would merely shine on their back.' His love does not change; it never ends. Our reception of His love may falter but His love does not fail.

Many Christians are disappointed when they do not receive any response from those they reach out to, but love does not look for something for itself. It is not self-seeking. The church is not a mutual admiration society where we love one another for the benefit it it brings. We love one another primarily because that is the new commandment that Jesus has given us (1 John 4:21). It is our love for one another that Jesus said would mark us out as His disciples (John 13:35). Unconditional love for one another should be our distinctive lifestyle.

Secondly, living a life of love means *committed love*. There are two kinds of love: love of the feelings and love of the will. Biblical love involves the latter. That means that we do not withdraw from relationships when difficulties come. It means that we choose to hold through in times of conflict and not withdraw from the relationship. 'If we are faithless, he will remain faithful' (2 Tim. 2:13). Disillusionment is an inevitable part of the process of getting to know one another. Dietrich Bonhoeffer, the German theologian and martyr, wrote, 'The sooner this shock of disillusionment comes to an individual and to a community, the better for both.'[3] When that time comes then we have the opportunity to really love. Love is a verb, not a feeling. 'Love', said Paul, 'always perseveres' (1 Cor. 13:7).

Thirdly, love involves *believing the best of each other*, not the worst. We choose to exercise a generous spirit and attitude. We do not keep a mental list of one another's wrongs. Instead of 'biting and devouring each other' (Gal. 5:15), we protect each other (1 Cor. 13:7). In short, a life of love means the devotion that Christ has shown to us being shown to one another (Rom. 12:10). Nothing must ever be allowed to bring separation between us. The church is therefore not built around a cause, or held together by programmes or common goals or agreed agendas, but should be held together by our love.

1. Marc Europe statistics.
2. Coates, Gerald, *Gerald Quotes* (Kingsway Publications,1984), p.79.
3. Bonhoeffer, D., *Life Together* (SCM, 1954)(seventh impression 1968), p. 15.

CHAPTER 2

THE CHURCH—THE FELLOWSHIP OF THE HOLY SPIRIT

It is essential that we understand the environment described in the previous chapter. It is the environment of the church of Jesus. Without that understanding we are likely to misunderstand the spirit and the heart of Jesus' teaching to His disciples recorded in Matthew chapter 18.

Our understanding of His teaching is also likely to be limited if we have not grasped the fundamental nature of church. Paul told the church at Corinth, 'You are the body of Christ and each one of you is a part of it' (1 Cor. 12:27). The body of Christ is not a metaphor but an analogy. The church is not *like* a body, it *is* a body. It was for the apostle an organism, as opposed to an organisation: an organism that throbbed with the risen life of Jesus. The church is not therefore an isolated collection of individuals who recite the same creed or meet together in the same building, but they are essentially one body of people, united by one spirit and confessing one Lord (1 Cor. 12:13; Eph. 4:4, 5).

In the New Testament the Greek word *koinonia* further explains the nature of the church. The word signifies a common or shared life. The shared experience of the early Christian community was in and through the rich life of the Holy Spirit (2 Cor. 13:14; Acts 2:42). The early Christians were one in heart and mind and their relational unity was a unique feature of their life together. It was this fact that explains why, at the time of the Reformation, Martin Luther made a very important distinction between the church and the institution of his day. Luther preferred to use the word 'congregation' rather than 'church' because to him the church was not an 'it' or a thing but a unity of persons. The church he saw in the Bible was a living body with a living head.

The theologian Emil Brunner has commented, 'We must not rationalise this concept of the body by reducing it to a mere metaphor . . . it is the mystery of the *ecclesia* as *the fellowship of the Spirit* that it has an articulate living order without being legally organised.'[1] The church is a living fellowship of people being built together in relationship by Christ Himself. Paul can therefore say, 'And in him you too are being built together to become a dwelling in which God lives by his Spirit'(Eph. 2:22).

Fellowship is much more than sharing friendship together, because there is an inevitable cleansing effect in real fellowship. John records that fellowship with one another and the cleansing of our sins by the blood of Jesus are conditional upon walking in the light (1 John 1:7). God loves us unconditionally, but that does not mean He will fellowship with us unconditionally. In 1 John 1:6 we read, 'If we claim to have fellowship with him yet walk in the darkness, we lie.' Richard Exley, pastor and broadcaster, states, 'God's model: unconditional love, conditional fellowship.'[2]

God's model is therefore also our model. In our relationships together we have a responsibility not just to create an environment of acceptance, encouragement, openness and honesty but also, at times, to admonish, correct and bring discipline to our fellow believer. It is all part of fellowship. Fellowship involves a cleansing environment.

Fellowship is a cleansing environment but also one that avoids legalism. Gerald Coates once shocked his listeners by announcing, 'This is a church that allows people to sin.' What he was saying was that we do not want an environment in church life and relationships where people have to hide from one another for fear of being discovered. In an environment where we fear discovery, sin will lie hidden, covered up and even denied.

In some churches Christians appear horrified at the thought that a real sinner might be discovered amongst them. We do not want churches living in unreality and denial. We want an environment where we love one another enough and are faithful enough to help one another walk in the light with God and one another. Sin is not a problem to God because He has made provision through His Son. It should not be a problem to us. In the light sin can be forgiven, cleansed and put out of sight.

The heart of the Gospel is all about restored fellowship. The Good News is that God has reconciled us to Himself (2 Cor. 5:19). He has won us over into fellowship with Himself. He has reconciled us not only to Himself but also to one another (Eph. 2:16). That is why anything that cuts across what God has done is taken very seriously in the Bible. Gossip and divisiveness, for example, are spoken about in very clear terms. Proverbs 16:28 says that 'a gossip separates close friends' and gossips are included in the same list as those who practise wickedness (Rom. 1:29–30). We are also warned that we should have nothing to do with a divisive person (Titus 3:10). In fact we should watch out for those who cause division (Rom. 16:17). These things go straight against the very heart of the Gospel message. They divide the church and break fellowship.

It is therefore important for us to understand not only the spirit of Jesus' words but also the context in which Matthew puts them in chapter 18. One of the first things to notice about the words of instruction is that they follow the parable of the lost sheep. Jesus has used this parable to underline the fact that people are precious to God. He hates to lose even one small sheep. However, as Ken Blue and John White have pointed out, we often focus our attention on the lostness of the single sheep rather than the fact that someone has been lost from the sheepfold.[3] The thrust of Jesus' teaching is that there are times when we lose fellowship with a brother or sister through sin. Sin affects our fellowship; it can cause 'little ones' to stumble. Through that sin the members of the community are the ones who lose something. Fellowship breaks down and we lose out.

Fellowship is a precious thing. It is highly valued by God and should be by the church. When we lose fellowship we should be anxious for it to be restored, like the shepherd who longs to find the lost sheep. The prime issue is not therefore the nature of the sin. The purpose of Jesus' teaching is to establish how we restore fellowship. He wishes to show us, as disciples, how we can imitate the Father's concern for the wandering sheep.[4] It is not a focus on the sin but the fact that a brother or sister needs to be won back into fellowship. Fellowship is the issue, not the gravity of the sin.

The sin that Jesus is talking about in Matthew 18:15 has to be anything, however small or large (in our own thinking), that causes a breach in fellowship. Sin always leads to a breakdown in relationship. When relationships are affected then our desire, like that of the shepherd, should be to put things right. Our goal is to win that brother or sister over—to fellowship with God and with fellow believers.

Jesus, therefore, is addressing the question of what we should do when relationships go wrong. He is instructing us as to what we should do if we see a brother or sister commit sin or we ourselves are sinned against. It needs to be pointed out that whether the sin is against us personally or otherwise is unimportant. In fact 'against you' does not appear in some of the Greek manuscripts. The important thing, as we have already seen, is that fellowship has been affected. Fellowship has been breached either between myself and another or between others that I have been a witness to.

It may be that I have been hurt by something someone did or said. My fellowship with that person has therefore been affected and I need to put it right. It may be that I have heard someone speak unkindly against someone else. The fact that I heard the unkind words now means that my fellowship with the speaker and with the person referred to has been affected. I cannot avoid my responsibility and therefore need to put it right.

Often people are unaware of the signs that we are out of fellowship with someone. Here are some of the signs that I suggest indicate that fellowship has broken down.

1. We begin to feel resentful towards someone. We may feel let down by them or that they have broken trust between us. We sense that they owe us something—at least an apology!
2. Hearing the person's name produces a reaction

within us. It is not a good feeling. If we had the opportunity to pray with someone they would certainly not be our choice. We would certainly not be able to break bread with them.

3. We find it difficult to speak well of the person. If we do speak well of them we are anxious to add a telling 'but'. We do not really think that they can be fully trusted.

4. The temptation to talk to others about them is very strong. We need others to be aware of what we think we know about them. We are tempted to find others who will agree with us about this person.

5. We tend to ignore the person concerned and definitely avoid eye contact. Eyes are the telling window of the soul. When we are in fellowship together we can look one another straight in the eye. We should have nothing to hide.

6. Our conscience leaves us a little uneasy. We probably feel the need to justify ourselves.

7. Our fellowship with the individual is deliberately kept shallow. We are uncomfortable at talking about deeper and more personal things.

8. We cannot ask God to bless them. We want Him to judge them.

9. Over and above all these things, broken fellowship affects our worship. In Matthew 5:23 Jesus said: 'If you are offering your gift at the altar and there remember that your brother has something against you, leave your gift there in front of the altar. First go and be reconciled to your brother; then come and offer your gift.' When that awareness drops into our mind we are not told to resist condemnation or rebuke the devil or try and forget about it. We must leave our worship and put things right.

Unresolved issues cannot be swept under the carpet because the Holy Spirit will not allow it.

Let us summarise the sin that Jesus is talking about. Firstly, it may be sin that has been directed at us. We have personally been sinned against. Secondly, it may be that you have been accused of sinning against another. In the words of Matthew 5:23, 'Your brother has something against you.' Thirdly, we may be the witness of sin that is not directed against us, but is nevertheless damaging to the individual or individuals involved.

In every case the salient fact is that fellowship has been affected. The harmony and unity that characterise fellowship have been broken. It can no longer be said that we are of one heart and mind.

1. Brunner, Emil, *The Misunderstanding of the Church* (Lutterworth, 1953) p. 53.
2. Exley, Richard, *Perils of Power* (Honor Books, 1988), p. 106.
3. White, J. and Blue, K., *Healing the Wounded* (Inter-Varsity Press, 1985), p. 88.
4. France, R.T., *Matthew: Tyndale Bible Commentaries* (Inter-Varsity Press, 1989), p. 274.

CHAPTER 3

THE CHURCH—THE RECONCILED COMMUNITY

The church is the community of those that have been reconciled to God and reconciled to one another. Therefore, when we feel that we have been sinned against personally or see a brother or sister commit a sin that affects our fellowship together, Jesus gives us some very clear steps and instructions as to what we should do. The steps are directed towards reconciliation—being brought back together.

In order to be as clear and as practical as possible I am setting out the steps we should take in this and the next two chapters.

STEP ONE : 'Go.'

In Matthew 18:15 Jesus begins by firmly placing the responsibility with the individual—'You go.' He makes the issue our personal responsibility. I have to go, not someone else but me. Secondly, we go to show our fellow believer his fault. The Greek verb which is here translated 'to show fault', in Ephesians 5:13 is translated 'expose'.('Everything exposed by the light becomes visible.') This conveys the exact purpose of our going. We are not prejudging the issue but we do want to bring the whole situation into the light and expose it, to see it for what it is.

It is at this first step that Christians usually find any number of excuses for not going. They can think of a thousand reasons why this does not apply to them.

Here are some of the excuses we make.

1. 'I'll wait for them to come to me.'

No, that is no excuse. Jesus clearly said, 'You go.' There is no need to wait. The person concerned may never come to you and probably never will. Quite simply, they are not the offended party. If they were aware of their sin they might well have put it right already, but they have not. The other person might well be totally unaware of their sin or offence.

If, on the other hand, we are aware that a brother or sister has something against us, then it will affect our worship until we go and see them (Matt. 5:23). We cannot worship God or break bread with one another when issues are outstanding between us. In either case Jesus says, 'You go.'

If we wait we could be waiting for a very long time. Just recently someone came to see me about a matter that happened over two years previously. Whilst the incident was very much alive in the mind and heart of the person who came to see me, I could not recall the incident. I was therefore unable to apologise or clarify the situation. The brother concerned was in the situation where he had dwelt upon and come to conclusions about an incident of which I was now totally unaware. If he had responded to the words of Jesus he would have come to see me immediately, and we could then have been reconciled. As it was, he needed to apologise for the resentment and mistrust that had built up on his side through a lack of openness and honesty about his feelings. He had not taken the first step Jesus asked of him.

2. 'It's wrong for me to judge other people.'

Well, that is true. Jesus did clearly teach that we should not judge others if we ourselves do not want to be judged (Matt. 7:1). However, we have to ask what He meant when He said we should not judge one another. He was in fact talking about an attitude that condemns others. Judgementalism jumps to hasty conclusions. It is a superior attitude that puts people in a box. It sees them as sinners who are never going to change. It is also an unforgiving attitude that prejudges the conclusion of the matter even before it has been discussed. The person with that attitude acts as judge and jury and delivers the verdict all in one go. The verdict is of course guilty!

Primarily Jesus is not asking us to go and judge our brother or sister. He is asking us to go and 'win' them. Until we go we do not know the conclusion or outcome. We go to establish fellowship.

Whilst it is clearly wrong to be judgemental, we are called to make judgements over sin issues. Those that are spiritual are called to 'make judgements about all things' (1 Cor. 2:15). In 1 Corinthians 5:12 Paul points out that it is not our business as Christians to judge those outside the church because that is God's province. However, he argues that inside the church we are called to judge. He goes on to say that we are one day going to judge angels, so we had better get some practice with people now.

3. 'I could be mistaken.'

Yes, of course you could be mistaken. If that is the case and there has been misunderstanding, then that will become clear. To be mistaken is not a problem. God wants us to be faithful to one another and will honour us for caring enough to go. If we prove not to be mistaken, then in turning someone from their sin we are highly commended (James 5:20).

4. 'I could offend the person.'

This excuse really means, 'There could be confrontation'. If we really have genuine love for our fellow believer then we will risk that possibility. No one enjoys confrontation. If we do then there is probably something wrong with our attitude. However, we have to face the fact that there can be no faithfulness without there being confrontation at times. A fear of confrontation is in fact not a weakness but a sin. It is a lack of faithfulness.

If a believer is offended by our faithfulness then he or she will probably need some help with his or her attitude anyway. Why should our kindness and care be offensive? Even if some form of correction proves necessary this doesn't have to involve confrontation. We often meet confrontation where there is defensiveness or pride. Seeing our brother does not have to be a heavy thing but a very natural expression of care.

5. 'I am inexperienced.'

We are all inexperienced until we gain experience. It is only by 'going' that we grow in confidence. Going to see our brother or sister does not have to be a tremendously formal occurrence. It can take place over a cup of coffee or in a private corner after a church meeting. It does not have to be made into something awesome. It should be a very natural part of our lives together. In the family situation it obviously takes place in the home.

6. 'I'll tell someone else—they can go.'

No, not someone else. There is a saying 'You cannot fire someone else's bullets.' Jesus said, 'You go.' 'You go' is in the singular tense in the Greek. No one else needs to know, not even for prayer. Often what is called 'sharing a need for prayer' is nothing less than gossip. It may be spiritualised gossip but it is nevertheless gossip.

Here Jesus puts in a warning against gossip and underlines His point by emphasising 'just between the two of you'. There is the possibility that the person we are going to see has not in fact sinned. In which case someone else now has a wrong perspective on that brother or sister which is going to affect their relationship with them. That's why Jesus says go alone. Others do not need to know, not even the pastor or leader. Involving others at Step One can be nothing but a gateway to gossip. Jesus places the responsibility on our shoulders alone.

7. 'I'm hurt but it doesn't matter.'

Yes, it does matter. It is often those very hurts that build up over a period of time and destroy relationships. If we are hurt by a brother or sister, even if the hurt was unintentional, then our fellowship with them has been affected. We need to repair the broken link. Going to see the person will be an important step in keeping our heart clear from resentment and bitterness.

It is fact of life that 'you cannot bury what is alive'. If we are carrying hurts that have not been expressed to the persons concerned, then those hurts and feelings that we carry will become ground for the enemy. Scripture tells us not to give the devil a foothold (Eph. 4:27). It is these very hurts that the devil will use to destroy our trust and love for one another. We can build up a view of others that may be totally unfounded, but because we have not been obedient to Jesus' command to 'go', we never hear the other side of the story. If we have been hurt by others then we must be faithful and share our hurt. In that way the devil is refused a foothold.

Often people say time will heal, but time does not heal anything.

8. 'It's their problem.'

No, it's now *your* problem. Yes, we are our brother's keeper. Whether they are a personal friend or not is also irrelevant.

9. 'I'm nervous about going.'

Yes, most of us feel similarly and it is good to know that we all face the same challenge. We also have similar fears, like, 'Am I making a mountain out of a molehill? Will I make the situation worse?' When we are nervous we learn to depend on God.

Jesus clearly teaches us to go. The excuses we look for do not let us off the hook! Hopefully, having been convinced that it is our responsibility to go, we now need to know *how* we should go. We will look at this in the next chapter.

CHAPTER 4

THE CHURCH—THE PLACE OF FORGIVENESS

The attitude in which we approach our fellow believer is as important, if not more important, than the fact that we go. It is worth emphasising that, practically speaking, the act of going to see someone does not have to be a very formal or over-serious occasion. It can take place very naturally in the course of our relationship.

Where and how we meet together should be as normal and natural as possible. Going to see our brother or sister may involve fellowship over a cup of coffee, or a chat together after a church meeting. If we do not naturally relate together in the course of life then it may involve a special visit to the person's home, or if that is not possible then, exceptionally, a telephone conversation or even a letter. If at all possible a face-to-face conversation is the ideal. An impersonal letter or telephone call does not help the process of fellowship and dialogue. It could in fact further distance the relationship. These means of communication are also easy excuses for avoiding face-to-face fellowship.

Having committed ourselves to go, the first thing to grasp is that *we go in humility*. We must always bear in mind that we may be mistaken. There is always another side to what we hear or see. Not everything is as black or white as it first appears. That is why a sense of *vulnerability* is also important. We are not going to sort the person out, to put them right or to patronise them. We approach them in humility and vulnerability because we ourselves are subject to the same temptations to sin. We are not asked to correct one another from a position of arrogant moral superiority. In the same way that we encourage one another's strengths, we need to be equally faithful when we see a brother or sister fail. Correcting one another should be in the same spirit in which we teach one another (Col. 3:16). In other words, we have one another's best interests at heart.

In Galatians 6:1 Paul teaches that if someone is caught in a sin, that person should be restored *gently*. People are precious to God and restoration to fellowship needs a gentle and caring attitude. A condemning or heavy-handed attitude can cause as much damage as the sin itself. In this passage Paul then adds 'but watch yourself or you also may be tempted'. It is a warning and reminder that none of us are above or exempt from the same temptations to sin. In the words of Jude 23 we 'show mercy mixed with fear'.

Secondly, when we go, *we go forgiving*. It was after Jesus had given these words of instruction to His disciples that Peter asked Him the question as to how often we should forgive our brother. Peter thought seven times was generous but Jesus gave 490 times as a reasonable guideline!

Forgiveness runs at the frontier of God's love. He never stops forgiving. That is why when we fail to forgive we destroy the channel through which God's love comes to us. We have adopted an attitude that is the opposite to God Himself. If we do not have a forgiving attitude we can no longer represent God's heart to one another. In fact we are doing ourselves serious damage.

Following Peter's question about how often we should forgive, Jesus taught the parable of the unforgiving servant. In the story the jailors end up torturing the man who will not forgive his debtors. This is despite the fact that he himself has been forgiven an enormous debt. With chilling impact Jesus concludes the story in Matthew 18:35: 'This is how my heavenly Father will treat each of you unless you forgive your brother from the heart.'

When people first hear this teaching from Matthew 18 there are often those who like to play at being church. They see it as an ideal way of bringing pressure to bear on those they do not get on with too well. In one particular church there was a lady who, on hearing this teaching, went to see a fellow believer. On arriving at her house she sat down and presented her sister with a written list of all her faults and failings. Naturally the recipient of the list was quite devastated and had no idea how to respond. She felt as if she was being asked to justify her very existence!

Fortunately God does not deal with us like that, nor does He want us to deal with one another in that way. I am glad God does not wake us in the morning with a list of our sins from the previous day. He is a gracious God who is merciful and forgiving. When His Holy Spirit does bring conviction of sin, He does so one sin at a time and always gives the opportunity for immediate repentance and forgiveness.

And finally, when we go, we must keep reminding ourselves that *we go to win* our brother or sister. We are not going to win an argument but to win them back to a place of fellowship and openness and honesty. It is because we are going to win our brother or sister back into open fellowship that our attitude is so important. If we go with a 'holier than thou' attitude then we are likely to lose, not win them. If we are heavy-handed and condemning then we are also going to lose them. It is the Holy Spirit that brings conviction of sin, not us. That is not our role. We point out what we see as the fault but the Holy Spirit brings the conviction. When we try and play the role of the Holy Spirit then we can easily end up bringing a sense of unnecessary guilt and condemnation.

So then, let's return to Jesus' practical steps to win our brother or sister. Supposing we have now gone to win our fellow believer in an attitude of humility and forgiveness. Two results are possible. The first is that we win our brother or sister and fellowship is restored. If there was sin, then that sin has now been forgiven. This is the intended goal. It may be that restoration and ongoing care will be needed, but the issue itself has now been brought to a conclusion. However, supposing he or she 'refuses to listen' (Matt. 18:17)?

By this Jesus means us to understand that we encounter an attitude of heart. It is an attitude that communicates a mind that is already made up. The individual is not open to talk, or fellowship. To listen means to listen with an open heart and mind and to have a change of mind, if necessary. To listen reflects an honesty and willingness to learn. If we do not find that we are being listened to in this sense, then Jesus says we take Step Two. However, before we consider Step Two let us just briefly look at what is likely to follow 'if he listens'.

Where there has been sin and in order for fellowship to be restored, there are responses which we can reasonably expect.

1. Sin has to be acknowledged.

This means that responsibility is accepted and the sin named for what it is. Calvary does not cover what we have not first uncovered. Proverbs 28:13 says, 'He who conceals his sins does not prosper, but whoever confesses and renounces them finds mercy.' When someone says, 'I am sorry you got hurt', that is not confession and renunciation. Accepting responsibility means that I acknowledge that I caused the hurt by an attitude or sin for which I now need to ask forgiveness. People can feel hurt for all sorts of reasons, including an oversensitivity to others. The issue is whether the hurt was caused unnecessarily. If it was, then forgiveness needs to be asked for. Forgiveness can only be extended to the repentant heart. 'Repentance', says C. S. Lewis, 'is not something God demands of you before He will take you back and which He could let you off if He chose; it is simply a description of what going back is like.'[1]

2. Forgiveness has to be given.

Forgiveness means that we are saying that we choose not to remember the offence again. We are releasing the person from any sense of debt towards us. Forgiveness is important because it frees us from resentment which ultimately leads to bitterness, and this can affect others (Heb. 12:15).

In John 20:23 Jesus emphasises again the awesome responsibility of releasing people from their sins. He said to His disciples, 'If you forgive anyone his sins, they are forgiven; if you do not forgive them, they are not forgiven.' The Greek word translated 'not forgiven' implies that the sin still sticks to them. They are not loosed from their sins. Where we fail to forgive in response to genuine repentance we are in danger of the person's sin sticking to us.

We were once counselling a man who was struggling with a sense of living under constant disapproval. Many years earlier in his life it emerged that he had left a church under a sense of disapproval from the leader of that church. He was asked if he had forgiven that leader for the sense of injustice which he felt. He said he had, but when it was suggested that he verbalise again that forgiveness and pray for God's blessing on the man, he was unable to do so. The last thing he wanted was for God to bless him. He wanted God to judge him! After further counsel he realised that Jesus requires us to bless even our enemies, and that through his failure to forgive, that man's influence in his life was still oppressing him many years later. He had not loosed him from his sins and was consequently bound to them himself. He had become the prisoner Jesus warned about in the parable (Matt. 18: 23–35).

3. What was wrong needs to be put right.
Restitution is an important part of repentance. We are not talking about penance where we have to earn the right to be forgiven, but we can expect repentance to produce fruit (Matt. 3:8). If a person has been involved in the sin of gossip, then it is not unreasonable that the individual should go back to those that have been the subject of gossip and acknowledge his or her sin.

4. Restoration should follow reconciliation.
Often sin leaves its scars and the enemy is always looking to exploit guilt and fear. We need to be aware that those who have been forgiven may need ongoing help, encouragement and pastoral care. It

may therefore be appropriate to suggest that they see the person with pastoral responsibility for them to receive whatever help is necessary. Restoration is a process of ongoing care and input.

But what if he or she will not listen? Jesus now suggests that a procedure begins which ultimately involves the church. In the next chapter we look at what it means for the church to be involved in resolving relationship conflict and sin.

---

1. Quoted in Exley, Richard, op. cit., p. 29.

CHAPTER 5

THE CHURCH—THE PLACE OF DISCIPLINE

STEP TWO : 'Take one or two others along.'

We are now faced with the fact that although we have been obedient to Jesus and talked to our fellow believer about the sin issue, they have not been willing to listen to us. At this stage we are asked to involve one or two others. The one or two that Jesus says should now come along with us are not allies on our side, but they are there as witnesses in order that 'every matter may be established'. This was a well-known principle to the disciples. It was taken from the Old Testament and had its roots in the law of Moses. Witnesses were called in a variety of circumstances, primarily to establish the truth of a matter. The role of a witness was twofold: firstly, to protect from wrongful accusation and secondly, to bring confirmation by way of judgement.

It is when we hear the word 'judgement' that we often get the wrong idea. We think of judgement in terms of punishment and being put right or sorted out. To bring judgement to a situation is quite simply to bring an assessment. If, for example, we believe that one day that we all have to sit before the judgement seat of Christ, this means that a day will come when we hear God's assessment of our lives. We will listen to His perspectives on the way we have lived rather than come to our own assessment or listen to the views of others.

The witnesses are therefore called to listen to both sides and then objectively assess the situation between the two believers. They are not there to bring more weight to the condemnation. Some people think of them as the heavy mob! They are certainly not that.[1] When fellowship breaks down, progress in a relationship comes to a halt. God wants us to go forward and witnesses, by bringing their assessment of the situation, do bring the seriousness of the situation to bear but more importantly, they also take the matter forward.

The witness of two or three is a binding principle in Scripture. If we cannot submit to the witness of two or three, then we either have a very stubborn heart or have become the victim of very unusual circumstances. The norm is that the witness of two or three establishes the matter. The writer of Ecclesiastes recognises that a threefold cord is not easily broken (Eccles. 4:12).

What therefore do we do if the person still will not listen? Jesus leaves us no alternative than to move on to a very serious step.

STEP THREE: 'Tell it to the church.'

The matter is no longer the concern of just two or three—the church is involved. The issue has to be heard by all. It means that the matter is no longer a private concern because there are implications for the whole group. When Jesus spoke these words, 'the church', at that time, could only have meant His disciples. The question therefore arises—which church do we tell it to? Based on Jesus' principle we have to say that it is the network of relationships with which the individual is associated.

For the twelve apostles there were probably occasions when they alone were implicated. Relationship difficulties between them were only appropriate for fellowship and discussion within that team. When the 72 disciples were sent on their church mission then it would seem that any serious issue arising would have been appropriate to that network. Likewise, following the Ascension of Jesus, we see from Acts 1:15 that a network of about 120 believers was involved in discussions about Judas. If a brother was not prepared to listen to the binding witness of two or three, then the implicated network needed to know and have the opportunity to make their feelings known.

It is important that a wider network is made aware of the situation and in particular that the matter does not remain the sole province of leadership. Unless the church members have the opportunity to hear the matter, they will be deprived of the responsibility that Jesus places on them to bring their corporate judgement.

Paul identified the same principle when he pointed out that 'there should be no division in the body, but . . . its parts should have equal concern for each other. If one part suffers, every part suffers with it; if one part is honoured, every part rejoices with it' (1 Cor. 12:25, 26). The church is more than its leadership and cannot escape the implications of an unrepentant member.

Again, as we saw earlier, it is not the nature of the particular sin that makes it necessary to tell it to the church. It is the hardened state of heart of the unrepentant person. Here we have a person who will not listen to his fellow believers. Here is someone who is not open to fellowship. All those who know the person or are involved in the same network of committed relationships therefore need to know the facts of the matter. It is unlikely that unrepentant individuals will want to stand before the church, but they obviously have the right to do so, to explain their perspective and submit themselves to the church.

But what if they still will not hear?

STEP FOUR: 'Treat him as you would a pagan or tax collector.'

This final step only acknowledges the lack of fellowship that already exists. There is now no place for fellowship. There is no further basis on which to appeal. Such a one has in fact cut himself off and excluded himself from fellowship. The church is only recognising what is a patent reality. The person is not interested in fellowship. He or she is acting and behaving like an unsaved person and is, as Paul was to say later of the divisive person, 'self-condemned' (Titus 3:11). An unrepentant person can only be treated as an outsider.

It needs to be said that some commentators do not see the appeal to the church as judicial at all. R.T. France comments, 'The church meets not to adjudicate a dispute, but for pastoral appeal.'[2] He even suggests that if the individual is unrepentant no disciplinary action should follow. He argues that because the Greek word for 'you' in Matthew 18:17 is in the singular, Jesus intends that only the aggrieved disciple should keep his distance from the unrepentant sinner.

We have to say that this is unthinkable. It

contradicts the very unity of the body of Christ. We cannot believe that Jesus could suggest that it was only for one disciple to break off fellowship and therefore fine for the rest of the church to eat and drink and share fellowship with the sinner. The whole church is now involved in the process. F. F. Bruce takes a different view from France and is clear that in this passage, as in John 20:23, we do have 'authority to exercise church discipline'.[3]

The way in which the church should treat the unrepentant is often misunderstood. Jesus did not hate pagans and tax collectors. He did not 'cold-shoulder' them. Jesus is saying that we should recognise that they are not part of the family of the church. The intimate fellowship of family relationships is not open to them. That is why we do not welcome such people into our homes (1 Cor. 5:11). Home is the place for family and intimacy. They are in that sense excluded from our homes; they are out in the cold—by choice.

It is however important to remember that the door to forgiveness is never closed. The reason we exclude such a person from fellowship is in fact in order that ultimately they may be won back to fellowship. There is nothing like the cold to remind someone with a heart of the warmth of family and God's love. There is no limit to the times we forgive repentant sinners. The only issue now is whether there will be complete repentance.

It is at this point in the narrative of Matthew 18 that Jesus speaks to His disciples and reminds them that the powers of the Kingdom are committed to His church. He speaks to them of the awesome authority of the church. A literal rendering of the Greek future perfect tense would be 'what you bind on earth shall have been bound in heaven: what you loose on earth shall have been loosed in heaven'. Heaven and earth are in harmony. What we together decided on earth, has in fact already been decided in heaven. Heaven is in on the side of the church!

When Jesus talks of 'binding' in this context it simply means to withhold fellowship. To 'loose' means to forgive and open a pathway to fellowship. Those sins and attitudes that are unacceptable in the church we 'bind', but those who repent of their sin we 'loose' from their sin.

Jesus underlines the awesomeness of what He has just said by emphasising the tremendous power of agreement. Where even two or three are met in Jesus' name, whatever they ask for in agreement together God will do it for them. He is again speaking about our responsibility to remove from fellowship those who refuse to repent, and the authority He has given us to forgive. Heaven is behind us in the decisions we make. Wherever two or three are in 'symphony'—that is the essence of the Greek word—then God honours that agreement.

---

1. France, R.T., Matthew. op. cit., p. 274. France suggests that the witnesses are 'to add force to the persuasion' but this prejudges the issue. As he rightly points out, they are not witnesses of the original offence anyway.

2. ibid., p. 275.

3. Bruce, F.F., Answers to Questions (Paternoster Press, 1972), p. 49.

CHAPTER 6

THE TROUBLE AT CORINTH

In the fifth chapter of 1 Corinthians Paul writes about his concern on two issues. The first is a blatantly immoral situation in the church where a man is having a sexual relationship with his father's wife. The second and apparently more important concern is the church's attitude toward the situation.

The apostle is clearly angry that this man had not been expelled from the church. Rather than being proud of themselves he wants to know, 'Shouldn't you rather have been filled with grief and have put out of fellowship the man who did this?'(1 Cor. 5:2). In effect Paul is saying that the church has been sinning by condoning the man's sin. They had failed to recognise the 'yeast principle' that eventually a little yeast will affect a whole batch of dough.

Gordon Fee comments, 'And it is precisely this failure to recognise the depth of their corporate sinfulness due to their arrogance that causes Paul to take such strong action.'[1] The whole church is in danger of being infected by this man's loose morality. The apostle is emphasising the principle of identification. The church is the community of the redeemed and cannot at the same time identify with the practice of sin. The same point is underlined in 2 John 10: 'If anyone comes to you and does not bring this teaching, do not take him into your house or welcome him. Anyone who welcomes him shares in his wicked work.' The church, by failing to dissociate itself from sin, identifies with it and thereby condones it.

Paul then goes on to clear up a misunderstanding. When he previously wrote and told the church not to associate with sexually immoral people, or the greedy, or idolaters, he was not referring to people in the world. He expected Christians to mix with such people in the world.

The issue is that anyone calling himself a 'brother' (meaning a believer) cannot carry on living as a drunkard or a swindler and continue to regard himself as part of the fellowship of the church. It is not only sexual sin that calls for discipline, but he argues, 'You must not associate with anyone who calls himself a brother but is sexually immoral or greedy, an idolater or a slanderer, a drunkard or a swindler. With such a man do not even eat.' Any believer who wilfully and proudly practises sin as a lifestyle cannot escape the judgement of the church.

Following the logic of Jesus' teaching in Matthew 18 Paul calls for the church to exercise its responsibility and bring judgement to the situation (1 Cor. 5:12). The man's sin was already public knowledge and therefore his discipline was also to be public. The practical steps for removing this man from fellowship are outlined.

Firstly, it is when the church are together in the name and power of the Lord Jesus that discipline is to be brought (1 Cor. 5:4). Here Paul is recalling the words of Jesus in Matthew 18:20: 'For where two or three come together in my name, there am I with them.' To the Jews, ten was the minimum gathering required to constitute a synagogue. However the Jews also believed that wherever two or three gathered to speak the words of the Torah, there the Shekinah glory (the Holy Spirit) was present.[2] Jesus took this well-known saying and suggested that where two or three are gathered in His name, then He Himself will be present in the power of the Holy Spirit. His Spirit will undergird the authority of His words. Paul also reminds the church not to forget that although not with them physically, he is nevertheless with them in spirit and wants his apostolic presence amongst them to be felt and honoured (1 Cor. 5:3). As well as fulfilling the commands of Christ, the church will also be outworking the apostolic doctrine. The apostle is therefore requiring that the church gather with a clear sense of purpose, on the authority of Christ's word, and under the anointing of the Holy Spirit.

Secondly, in the phrase 'hand this man over to Satan' (1 Cor. 5:5) we have another description of what Jesus meant by treating an unrepentant sinner as a pagan and tax collector. These equally stark and chilling words are used to convey the seriousness of what is taking place. 'To hand over to Satan' is another description of what it means to be put out of fellowship. The church is a place of protection and salvation under the Lordship of Jesus, but outside is the province of Satan. In Acts 26:18 we read that salvation involves turning 'from darkness to light, and from the power of Satan to God'. In Colossians 1:13 similarly the process is described: 'For he has rescued us from the dominion of darkness and brought us into the kingdom of the Son he loves, in whom we have redemption, the forgiveness of sins.' To be excluded from fellowship, where sin remains bound and unforgiven, is simply to be transferred back to the kingdom of darkness and to the province of the 'god of this age' (2 Cor. 4:4).

In this passage from 1 Corinthians we also have a very clear description of the purpose of the discipline. Here the effect, but not the ultimate goal, is the destruction of 'the sinful nature' (or 'flesh', KJV). Hopefully the severe discipline will destroy the appetite for his fleshly way of living. Unrestrained sin can quickly destroy an appetite for sin or even lead to death. The goal of the discipline is that the man will come to his senses, like the prodigal son in the parable, and once more return to fellowship. It is important to see that the purpose is redemptive. The objective is not the destruction of his spirit but of his flesh life, in order that 'his spirit [might be] saved'. The experience of living again in the world, outside the fellowship and community lifestyle of the church, is intended to lead the sinner to repentance. The sinner has lessons to learn in the school of Satan. He will not learn from the church, but hopefully he will learn from his experience in the world.

Paul wrote to Timothy of Hymenaeus and Alexander who were two people 'whom I have handed over to Satan to be taught not to blaspheme' (1 Tim. 1:20). Whether they learned their lesson Paul does not say, nor do we know if they lived or died. However we do know of several examples in the New Testament where God's direct intervention and discipline of believers was extremely sharp. Ananias and Sapphira lied about the money they had put into the offering and were both carried out of the house dead (Acts 5:1–10). The newly baptised Simon feared the same fate (Acts 8:24). In Corinth itself Paul suggests that some had actually died as a result of coming under God's judgement, through failing to recognise the body of the Lord (1 Cor. 11:30).

I myself know of a contemporary situation where a single believer chose to go and live with a married woman. An elder from the believer's church went to see him to warn him of the serious nature of his sin. The believer acknowledged his sin according to the teaching of Scripture but would not repent. At a gathering of the church he was therefore put out of fellowship. The church was shocked and sobered to hear a few months later that at the age of 40 he had died of a heart attack.

The harsh words of discipline used in the first Corinthian passage have raised for some the question as to whether a person handed over to Satan will in fact ultimately be saved. The first thing to be clear on is that *repentance will always lead to forgiveness and salvation*. That, as we have emphasised, is the objective of discipline. In 2 Corinthians 2:4–11 we have an example of a sinning believer coming to repentance. This was the result of discipline brought by the church. Some have suggested that here we have the same man who was living with his father's wife. However most commentators regard this as unlikely. The matter is unimportant. What we learn from this passage is that the church had brought discipline, as Paul had required, but had now gone overboard. The man was clearly repentant but they had failed to forgive him and re-affirm their love for him. They had strayed from licence to legalism. The majority, by which we may understand the consensus of the church, had presumably delivered the man to Satan but now Satan was in danger of taking advantage of them all. Through an unwillingness to forgive they were about to fall into one of Satan's traps.

Secondly, we have to be equally clear that *a

sinful lifestyle cannot bring any assurance of ultimate salvation (1 Cor. 6:9, 10). Having said this the Bible is silent on the issue of whether Ananias or Sapphira were ultimately saved and in the case of those who had died in Corinth Paul says, 'When we are judged by the Lord, we are being disciplined so that we will not be condemned with the world' (1 Cor. 11:32). Here at least he implies hope that these deceased believers will not ultimately be condemned. In 1 John 5:16 the writer states, 'If anyone sees his brother commit a sin that does not lead to death, he should pray and God will give him life. I refer to those whose sin does not lead to death. There is a sin that leads to death. I am not saying that he should pray about that.'

Some commentators have seen in the reference to a 'sin that leads to death' the persistent sinner who, having been excluded from fellowship, cannot be brought back to repentance and forgiveness.[3] The apostate ex-believer is therefore ultimately lost. Hebrews 6:4–6 certainly suggests that there are those who cannot be brought back to repentance. James also talks of 'saving from death' the brother who is brought back from wandering (James 5:20) and 2 Peter 2:20 says that those who have escaped the corruption of the world by coming to a knowledge of Jesus, and who then get entangled again in its corruption, are worse off at the end than if they had never known the way of righteousness.

In conclusion we have to say that Paul spoke of the act of putting someone out of fellowship in the gravest of terms. There can be no assurance for those whose sins are 'bound' by the church that they will be viewed any differently by heaven. To be outside the fellowship of church is not a safe place to be. Ultimately, however, we have to remember God is everyone's judge and to

Him we all have to give account. Not everything that calls itself the church is so viewed by God. To those therefore who feel themselves victims of authoritarian or abusive practice, He alone is our ultimate judge.

1. Fee, Gordon D., *The First Epistle to the Corinthians, The New International Commentary on the New Testament* (Eerdmans, 1987), p. 203.
2. Sigal, Phillip, *Judaism: The Evolution of a Faith* (Eerdmans, 1988), p. 98.
3. Bruce, F. F.(Ed), *The International Bible Commentary* (Marshall Pickering, 1986), p. 1585.

CHAPTER 7

THE IMPORTANCE OF CORRECTIVE DISCIPLINE

We have seen from the teaching of Jesus that corrective discipline is not the exclusive province of leadership. It is the church that is called to disciple the church. Leaders do have particular responsibilities in this area, as we shall see later, but Jesus firmly places the responsibility on every believer.

The Greek word which is often translated in the New Testament either as 'admonish' or 'warn' means 'to train by word'. It seeks to correct wrong thinking and improve the spiritual attitude. It contains the thought of correcting what is amiss.[1] We are all involved in admonishing and warning whether we are leaders or not. In Romans 15:14 (KJV) Paul regards all the church as competent to 'admonish one another'. He writes to the Colossians, 'Let the word of Christ dwell in you richly as you teach and admonish one another' (Col. 3:16). Similarly in 1 Thessalonians 5:14 it is not leaders that he is telling to 'warn those who are idle' but church members.

Corrective discipline is and has been a controversial practice in church history. Correcting fellow believers is controversial, firstly because *it does acknowledge our responsibility toward each other*. It underlines the relational nature of the church. In Romans 12:5 Paul writes, 'So in Christ we who are many form one body, and each member belongs to all the others.' If we belong to the body of Christ, which is the church, then we also belong to one another. Membership of the church is a costly business because it makes demands on our relationships.

Paul reminds us that in the body of Christ there is an interdependence and interrelatedness from which we cannot escape. Our interrelatedness involves a responsibility to each and every member. The answer to Cain's question, 'Am I my brother's keeper?' is an undoubted 'yes'! Perhaps not surprisingly in the New Testament we find the Greek word *allelon* translated 'one another' over 71 times. We are encouraged to love one another, to be devoted to one another, to honour one another, to serve one another, to submit to one another, to encourage one another and to build each other up, just to quote a few examples. One thing is clear—we cannot ignore one another.

The relational nature of the church is also underlined by Paul's description of the church of Christ as a body. In Ephesians 4:15–16 we read, '. . . speaking the truth in love, we will in all things grow up into him who is the Head, that is, Christ. From him the whole body, joined and held together by every supporting ligament, grows and builds itself up in love, as each part does its work.'

If we are going to grow up into the maturity of our head, then firstly, every member needs a relationship with the head. Our priority in relationship is always with the head—Christ Himself. Only in Him are we related and joined together. He is both the source of the nourishment on which the body lives and the source of its unity.

Secondly, every member has a part to play in the building up of the church. This is particularly brought out in Colossians 2:19 (NKJV) where we read again of 'the Head, from whom all the body, nourished and knit together by joints and ligaments, grows with the increase that is from God'. God has designed that our relationships together are in effect the channels of supply to the strength and unity that flows from the head. Only as we are knitted together and play our part will the church grow. At Colossae there were those who had lost contact with the head and consequently lost contact with the body as well. In isolation few are capable of perfect self-discipline. Relationships bring a discipline to our lifestyle and we must be grateful for them.

The second reason I would suggest corrective discipline has been controversial is that *it touches upon some of our fears*. Often in people's thinking correction is identified with confrontation. Most of us do not enjoy confrontation and some positively fear it. In fact if at all possible most of us try and avoid it. It was therefore a wise person who said, 'Whilst the church cannot be built on confrontation, neither can it be built without it.'

We also have fears in the area of accusation. Will we be accused of authoritarianism? Is this just another form of control? In fact we have to be honest and say that church history is littered with examples where precisely these things have taken place. We can read in the past of Zwingli encouraging the murder of the Anabaptists for heresy or of some present-day excesses in shepherding practices. However the church is and remains a voluntary society. Every individual has not only the right to join and submit themselves to the discipline of a church, but also the right to leave. No one can be forced to do anything against their conscience or choice.

In a certain church a member was asked, 'Who is there in your life who can make you do what you do not want to do?' The answer quite rightly came back: 'No one.' The questioner clearly had a misunderstanding of the issue of accountability in relationships. Accountability cannot be imposed upon anyone. We can only choose to submit ourselves and make ourselves accountable to others, willingly. The context has to be relationships of trust and mutual respect. Where this context is absent then every individual has the right to withdraw from fellowship and in doing so remove themselves from the discipline of a church.

The final reason why I would suggest corrective discipline arouses controversy is because *it involves the naming of sin*. The temptation in the church has been to prefer things swept under the carpet rather than exposed to the light. We have fears of being exposed ourselves as well as possibly seeing the exposure of others. Privately we may fear being hurt or even ending up disillusioned with others, maybe those whom we respect. Someone once said, 'The pious fellowship permits no one to be a sinner.' We would rather sin was not named. There are also dangers in the naming of sin. The sins of a more public and obvious nature like sexual sin or alchohol abuse can be magnified, but attitudes like pride and materialism can go unchallenged.

Although discipline is controversial, the consequences where churches fail to exercise it are enormous. Relationships either remain at a very superficial level or break down altogether. Churches that are in effect only preaching centres will remain largely unaffected. However in churches that strive after a body life undisciplined gossip can be particularly destructive. Leaders will ultimately fail to hold respect and factions and divisions will soon appear.

A failure to discipline can also have serious effects on new believers. If they come into a church where divisiveness, gossip, immorality and the like flourish, then they are unlikely to last long. The enemy will make sure that they too are picked off. The general results of a lack of discipline are a drain on pastoral ministry and a low-trust climate in which nothing good and wholesome can really flourish.

It is important we realise that as members of the church we are all called to discipleship. We are all called to follow Jesus. Corrective discipline is only one aspect of what it means to follow Him. If we are going to grow in character and maturity then we cannot avoid it. Corrective discipline is an essential and unavoidable part of a healthy church. Hopefully Jesus' words of instruction will only very occasionally lead all the way to Step Four, but if necessary our love for Jesus and His church will mean that we are prepared to take it that far. Faithfulness demands that we do so.

A Christian once had a vision of the church as a collection of diamonds and realised that God was communicating that He often sees us as uncut diamonds. To Him we are precious jewels who will one day make up His victory crown. But at this moment in time we are rough uncut diamonds, not the refined jewels that we will one day be. The person then asked God how we would get from being rough diamonds to the jewels that God intends. God showed them that it is in relationship together that our rough edges are rubbed off. He has given us the church to hone us and shape us to be the people He wants us to be. He puts us with people that we may not naturally choose to be with but they are His choice. It is as we walk in faithfulness and obedience to all He has asked of us that we will ultimately become the church that He wants us to be.

1. Morris, Leon, *Romans* (Eerdmans, 1988), p. 509.

CHAPTER 8

RESPONDING TO DISCIPLINE

To many people the practice of admonishing and if necessary bringing correction seems a harsh thing. They can only understand it in negative rather than positive terms. Discipline is in fact the cost of love. It is not the opposite of love. It was the theologian Bonhoeffer who underlined the fact that in the redeemed community of the church correction is not an option, but God's Word demands it. He writes: 'Nothing can be more cruel than the tenderness that consigns another to his sin. Nothing can be more compassionate than the severe rebuke that calls a brother back from the path of sin.'[1]

Our definition of love often excludes discipline but only because we have a weak view of love. Discipline and love go hand in hand. The proverb states, 'Better is open rebuke than hidden love. Wounds from a friend can be trusted' (Prov. 27:5,6). What the proverb is saying is that hidden love is no love at all. Love is an active thing that at times may have to risk losing us in order to win us. Receiving correction can be a painful experience but especially for our pride. If we are to be wounded, far better in the house of our friends than our enemies. Our friends are going to tell us the truth because they love us; our enemies will not have the same motive! As someone has rightly said, 'Truth will always set you free but first of all it will make you miserable.'

God disciplines us because He loves us—not for any other reason (Heb. 12:6). If we love one another there are times when discipline will be necessary. We need to realise that discipline and punishment are not the same. 'Punishment focuses on past mistakes, while discipline focuses on correct future behaviour.'[2] Discipline has the future in view and in that sense is redemptive. It seeks to change our future behaviour through the healing experience of discipline.

So often we think of discipline in terms of punishment, yet those who have been through times of discipline often speak of the sense of security and healing that the experience brought them. It was the faithful love of friends who did not reject them in their difficulties, but nevertheless were prepared to be honest with them, that imparted a sense of belonging they had not felt before. Now, rather than feeling threatened by the thought of being corrected, they actually feel secure in it—in the same way that a child does with a good father. It was T. S. Eliot who is reported often to have said, 'Oh for the comfort, the inexpressible comfort of feeling safe with a person.' In the church, safety is not the absence of discipline but the security of knowing that it is there.

In a passage on the theme of discipline (Heb. 12:5–12) the writer to the Hebrews identifies two wrong responses to discipline. Whilst he particularly has in mind the discipline of circumstances, the principles apply to all forms of correction and discipline. The first wrong response is to *make light* of discipline and treat it in a very offhand sort of way. This is often where God's hand behind the discipline is not perceived. We fail to treat it seriously because we fail to see God in it. The second is the opposite extreme where we *lose heart* completely. We allow the experience to crush us out of all proportion to God's intention for us. He wants us to respond and be healed but we are determined to be hurt!

In my own experience I have seen both responses. There are those to whom corrective discipline is brushed off very quickly and few lessons are learned. On the other hand there are those who immediately write themselves off completely and decide that God made a mistake in taking them on in the first place. They feel they might as well give up now because they are always getting it wrong. Self-pity quickly takes over from feelings of remorse. We have to encourage such people that when He died on Calvary Jesus already knew the very worst about us. His discipline is all part of His healing process for our lives.

The Hebrew passage outlines the positive response to discipline that God is looking for. Firstly, we are not being asked to be unrealistic. 'No discipline seems pleasant,' says the writer, 'but painful.' None of us enjoy it but as the proverb says, 'He who hates correction is stupid'(Prov. 12:1). Discipline is a learning experience. 'For those who have been trained by it' discipline produces a 'harvest of righteousness and peace'. The Greek word translated 'trained' in this passage is the word from which we derive 'gymnasium'. The writer is saying that discipline is all part of God's training ground, His gymnasium to keep us fit spiritually. Only illegitimate children fail to receive the privilege.

It is so easy to lose the heart and spirit of what Jesus is teaching. Outside the context of committed and caring relationships the church can easily lurch between licence and legalism. A church that does not respond to sin in its midst will soon lose the sense of security that comes from belonging together. The church will no longer be a place of safety.

When Paul wrote his first letter to the church at Corinth he was dismayed that a person practising immorality had not been put out of fellowship (1 Cor. 5:2). He told the church to gather together in Jesus' name and 'hand this man over to Satan so that the sinful nature may be destroyed and his spirit saved on the day of the Lord'. This sounds very frightening and Paul intended it to be taken very seriously. The church is a place of protection from the enemy. When we escape the kingdom of darkness we come into safety of the kingdom of God's Son. However, the church can never be a safe haven for unrepentant sinners.

Paul demands that the church should no longer protect this man but isolate and expose his sin. He needs to be seen for what he is. Either he is a redeemed person, in which case he will come to repentance through the experience and his spirit be saved, or he will be lost and proved unredeemed. This will be the opportunity to see what is really in his heart. He will show his true colours.

John reminds his churches that there were some people who had left them 'but they did not really belong to us. For if they had belonged to us, they would have remained with us' (1 John 2:19). Paul is saying the same thing to Corinth about this immoral person. In effect he is saying, 'Either he is part of you or not, but excluding him from fellowship will reveal the matter.' He clearly places the responsibility on the church to bring their judgement on the situation (1 Cor. 5:12). It needed resolution and a swift conclusion.

In his second letter to Corinth Paul refers to a situation where discipline had been brought to a man but now the church had gone overboard in the opposite direction. The man was now clearly repentant but the church were still standing clear of him. He needed comfort and reassurance but the church were failing to express the love he needed. They had forgotten the reason for expelling him from fellowship in the first place.

As Paul explained, the man now needed reassuring of their love (2 Cor. 2:8). His sin had not led to death (1 John 5:16), but their judgement had proved a decisive point in his redemption. He was now penitent and needed loosing from his sin and given opportunity to enjoy the wonderful forgiveness of God. He was a genuine brother who, through the discipline of the church, had returned to the fold. The church at Corinth had failed in their attitude and spirit towards him.

We can see a similar situation in 2 Thessalonians 3:15 where Paul warned of the danger of losing the compassion of God's heart towards those who are stumbling. The apostle says that those who are disobedient towards the instructions in his letter should not be associated with, in order to bring them to a sense of shame over their sinful ways. However he reminds the believers to make sure that their attitude is right. We are dealing with these people in such a way because they are brothers, not enemies. Paul says, 'Do not regard him as an enemy, but warn him as a brother.'

Our goal is to evoke a response from the brother. The response we are looking for is a changed attitude which will come from those of a humble heart. However where such a response is not forthcoming then, in Jesus' words, such a brother should continue to be treated as a 'pagan and tax collector'.

1. Bonhoeffer, D., op. cit., p. 83.
2. Exley, Richard, op. cit., p. 99.

CHAPTER 9

LEADERSHIP AND RESPONSIBILITY

Leadership is a gift, a responsibility and also a position of trust. Leaders therefore need to be ready to give an account (Heb. 13:17) of the way in which they teach and practise church discipline. The teaching of the Lord and His apostles is certainly not a legal code nor was it intended to develop into an ecclesiastical court system.

Legalism and insensitivity to the Holy Spirit is always a danger where discipline is divorced from the context of relationship. Emil Brunner, the theologian, identified the attraction of legalistic thinking when he wrote, 'It is so much easier to secure the life of a fellowship . . . by means of solid legal forms, by organisations and offices, than it is to allow the life of communion to be continually poured upon me . . . You can handle and shape as you please such things as law and organisation but you cannot act thus towards the Holy Ghost.'[1]

We cannot short-circuit the importance of our dependence on the wisdom and help of the Holy Spirit. In the New Testament we see a developing response to specific relationship problems that arose in the growing church. It was the teaching of Jesus that laid the foundation which the apostles, under the inspiration of the Holy Spirit, later developed and applied.

In the history of the church there have been two traditional approaches to the need for discipline. Firstly, discipline has been seen as necessary in order *to maintain the purity of the church*. If the church comprises God's holy people (Eph. 5:2) then not all forms of behaviour can be acceptable. The church must be a reflection of the desire of Christ for a spotless and radiant bride. It must be seen as the community of light and not of darkness. Secondly, discipline has been practised *to restore sinners from the error of their sins*. The concern here is not solely for the reputation of the church but also the righteousness of the individual and their standing before God. The goal is to see a change of heart and attitude in the sinner.

The authors Blue and White have added two more equally if not more important considerations.[2] Firstly, they emphasise the reconciliation of the sinner not just to God but also into fellowship and relationship. Friendship and intimacy within the body of Christ must also be restored. Indeed they see this as a prime motivation in bringing the sinner to repentance, namely the desire for the blessing which friendship with God and one another brings.

Secondly, the authors stress the need to bring healing and freedom to those restored. Inappropriate discipline or discipline poorly handled can harden hearts, not change them. What is needed is discipline that sets free. Discipline must bring freedom from the demonic, darkness and guilt, the fear of discovery, and legalism. Leaders therefore need to be clear on the primary purpose of discipline. It is not to purge the church of unsatisfactory members or to keep it looking respectable and outwardly pure while it is inwardly rotten. Reconciliation and restoration has to be the focus and goal.

Leaders have a responsibility to set an example to the church. They are not called to lord it over the church but to set the example (1 Peter 5:3). In that sense they exist to create the climate of the church. Just as leaders are called to teach, they also have a responsibility to admonish. Admonishing and teaching are seen as complimentary in Colossians 1:28. They are two sides of the same coin and should be conducted in the same spirit. Teaching involves the impartation of positive truth. Admonition or, as it is sometimes translated, warning, relates to what is wrong and needs to be put right. They are both for the training of individuals. In fact Scripture itself, our teaching authority, is 'useful for teaching, rebuking, correcting and training in righteousness' (2 Tim. 3:16). It is also arguable from 1 Thessalonians 5:12 that admonition is a particular mark of leadership. Timothy certainly is exhorted by the apostle to 'correct, rebuke and encourage—with great patience and careful instruction' (2 Tim. 4:2). Titus also is told to 'encourage and rebuke with all authority' (Titus 2:15).

The maxim that leaders must always adopt is 'rebuke but do not reject'. In teaching and admonition the total acceptance of the individual is paramount. As teachers in these things we are accountable to God and indeed can expect to be judged the more strictly (James 3:1). Discipline should never used as a form of control or persuasion. Tom Marshall quotes Menno Simons, the founder leader of the Mennonites, saying,

'Spiritual authority is never to make the rebel conform; its only purpose is to enable the obedient person to live a holy life. Therefore it rests on submission and obedience freely given. Furthermore, spiritual authority has only spiritual means at its disposal; its only weapons are prayer, scripture, counsel and the power of a holy life.'[3] Leadership demands therefore moral superiority.

The teaching of the New Testament also places a responsibility on leadership to bring ultimate discipline for the protection of the church. They must not step back from this obligation through a fear of being labelled authoritarian. Scripture frequently warns of wolves in sheep's clothing who will not spare the flock. The shepherd's role is to protect the flock from destructive influences both outside and within the fold.

Leadership accountability to the Word of God is seen in Titus 3:10 where the importance of dealing with divisive people is particularly underlined. 'Warn a divisive person once, and then warn him a second time. After that have nothing to do with him.' The root of the Greek word *hairetikos*, from which we get heretic, is 'choosing on his own'. Divisive people are fundamentally independent and genuine fellowship plays no part in their thinking. If independence as an attitude is not dealt with then party spirit will soon arise in the church.

Divisive people soon seek out others and when others of like attitude find one another, then rebellion is in the midst of the church. The sin of Korah becomes full blown (Jude 11). It is significant that Korah's rebellion began through an insistence on equality with leadership, followed by grumbling against leadership. Grumbling may seem an insignificant sin but Paul warns in 1 Corinthians 10:10 against this very attitude. The grumbling in Moses' camp was soon followed by accusations of leadership failure and authoritarianism (Num. 16:3, 11, 13).

Leaders can easily shrink back from their responsibilities because of a fear of being seen as authoritarian. On the contrary the role is a servant one. Again Dietrich Bonhoeffer says it so well, 'It is a ministry of mercy, an ultimate offer of genuine fellowship, when we allow nothing but God's Word to stand between us, judging and succouring. Ultimately we have no charge but to serve our brother, never to set ourselves above him, and we serve him even when we must speak the judging and dividing Word of God to him, even when in obedience to God we must break off fellowship with him.' He goes on to say, 'God's love ... breaks its way through to him only through judgement.'[4]

The principle of the destructive power of undisciplined sin is illustrated in Galatians 5:9: 'A little yeast works through the whole batch of dough.' Jesus used the image in a positive sense in Matthew 13:33 but the negative side is again referred to in 1 Corinthians 5:6. The church has an enemy in Satan who wants to infiltrate the church. If we know that God commands His blessing where brothers live together in unity (Ps. 133:1) then it should not surprise us that Satan wants to divide. He does it through encouraging divisive attitudes and talk.

Jesus did not shrink back from recognising him behind Peter's words (Matt. 16:23). Romans 16:17 also warns: 'Watch out for those who cause divisions.' The Greek word here implies a standing apart. Those who do not identify with the rest of the body often speak in terms of them and us. They speak of the church as something separate from them, not something of which they are a part. Leaders have a responsibility to guard the unity of the spirit.

Leaders should often ask themselves the question, 'If I were the enemy of this church how would I destroy its relationships?' The question was recently put to a group of young people who, along the lines of C. S. Lewis's Wormwood, came up with a strategy that they would use if they were Satan.

1. Create a low-trust climate. Tell people that trust is something they must earn, not something that is given. Sow little seeds of doubt in people's minds about the motives of other people. Do it over a long period of time but never be specific, just hint.
2. Question the integrity of leadership. Suggest that they too have feet of clay and infer that you know things that others do not. Refer to leadership in terms that imply they are set apart from the church of 'ordinary members'. Create the impression that they live in an ivory tower, not as one of the saints. Make them responsible for the things that go wrong.
3. Get the leaders themselves to stop sharing their hearts. Suggest to them that people would reject them if they knew what sins and temptations they struggled with. Get them eventually to the place where they deny that they ever have any problems. Remember, if you strike the shepherd the sheep will scatter.
4. Gossip maliciously about others. Spread half-truths about them but never total lies. Be subtle,

not obvious. Wherever possible divide. Whisper in people's ears that believing the best of people is naive. Never allow people to apologise to anyone.

It is the responsibility of leadership to teach the clear principles of Scripture to make sure that the church is not unaware of the enemy's schemes.

In 'binding and loosing' leaders have an important part to play alongside and at times representing and reflecting the mind of the church. There are two ways in which we see the function being exercised in the New Testament.

The phrase can mean firstly, *the function of forgiving or withholding forgiveness*. In Revelation 1:5 (in the Greek translation) we read, 'To him who loves us and has *loosed* us from our sins by his blood'. Jesus has wonderfully freed us from the penalty and sticking power of sin. Sin no longer sticks to the believer. Jesus, speaking to the disciples, says, 'Receive the Holy Spirit. If you forgive anyone his sins, they are forgiven; if you do not forgive them, they are not forgiven' (John 20:22, 23). Leon Morris points out that the Greek word translated 'not forgiven' or 'retained' in the King James version, implies the holding of something on to someone else.[5] The sin is bound to the person. They are not loosed from their sin, it still sticks. The church here has an awesome responsibility—that is why we need the Holy Spirit. As Morris says, the church acting under the Spirit will find that her decisions 'reveal what has already been determined in heaven'.[6]

Secondly, the phrase 'to bind and loose' can mean *to forbid or to permit*. The latter function was particularly exercised by the Jewish Rabbis through the Halakah. The Halakah spelt out the implications of the law for different situations and circumstances. It would appear that the elders and apostles were exercising a similar function in Acts 15 when they gave their ruling on the issue of the Gentile and Jewish communities. Paul suggests that in disputes between church members, particularly where legal consequences are threatened, even the least in the church can be appointed to act as judge over the issue (1 Cor. 6:4). Jesus has the function of binding and loosing in mind when in Matthew 23:13 he accuses the teachers of the law and Pharisees of shutting the kingdom of heaven in men's faces. 'You yourselves do not enter, nor will you let those enter who are trying to.' Permitting and forbidding can also be seen in the exercise of authority over demons and sickness. Jesus asks in Luke 13:16: 'Then should not this woman, a daughter of Abraham, whom Satan has kept bound for eighteen long years, be set free (loosed, KJV) on the Sabbath day from what bound her?'

The authority to bind and loose cannot be divorced from the Gospel. That is why leaders themselves are not exempt from correction and discipline themselves. They are subject to the same Gospel. When Peter preached to the Gentiles in the house of Cornelius he was exercising the keys of the kingdom (Matt. 16:19). The forgiveness of sins was extended to the Gentiles. However Peter himself was the subject of a public rebuke from Paul for compromising the very gospel he preached (Gal. 2:11).

In 1 Timothy 5:17–20 we see that an accusation against an elder follows the same procedure that Jesus outlined in Matthew 18. The confirmation of the two or three witnesses is needed before the accusation against an elder becomes a church matter. If sin is established then the discipline of leaders is also public and thereby demonstrates to the church that leadership is not a protected species. Leaders are servants and where they fail in that servant role they should be seen to be the same recipients of care, love and discipline that is afforded to other members. No more, no less.

1. Brunner, Emil, op. cit., p. 53.
2. White, J. and Blue, K., op. cit., p. 23.
3. Marshall, Tom, *Understanding Leadership* (Sovereign World, 1991), p. 111.
4. Bonhoeffer, D., op. cit., p. 83.
5. Morris, Leon, *John: New London Commentaries* (Marshall Morgan and Scott, 1973), p. 847.
6. ibid., p. 849.

CHAPTER 10

CONCLUSION: THE CHURCH—JESUS STYLE

The church of Jesus must be committed to a lifestyle that is a reflection of Jesus Himself. We have seen in the previous chapters that the apostles continually use Him as the supreme model whom we are called to follow. His lifestyle of love, acceptance, and forgiveness is seen as our example. Jesus also recognised His own need of others despite His unique relationship with the Father. Mark notes that Jesus chose His disciples first and foremost to be with Him (Mark 3:14). They learnt from Him the principles of relationship. They saw the way He related to family, friends and enemies and observed Him express both compassion and anger. They saw that He was not afraid to rebuke even in the strongest terms. How did poor Peter feel when Jesus rebuked his words as Satanic (Matt. 16:23)?

On the other hand they also saw His amazing capacity to forgive, even the very men who were crucifying Him. Peter knew the power of His love to restore even with a loving glance (Luke 22:61). Judas knew of His commitment to friendship even at the very point of betrayal (Matt. 26:50).

Jesus stands out for us as one who was

committed to relationship and committed to truth. The two were in harmony. One did not compromise the other. He was an example in speech, life, love, faith and purity (1 Tim. 14:12). Tom Marshall defines a relationship as involving four essential building blocks. They are trust, love, respect, and understanding.[1] Trust is the fundamental cost of committed relationships. It expresses the heart of the environment of the church that we looked at in the opening chapter.

The church needs to work continually at creating a high-trust climate. Trust is a choice and a risk that every relationship inevitably involves. Trust brings an accountability one to each other. It means a glad submission of ourselves to one another in the fear of the Lord (Eph. 5:21). The blessings of relationship are therefore not open to those who are not prepared for the cost and humility involved. Without trust friendship cannot be nurtured or grown.

The building block of Love has to be seen expressing itself in openness and transparent honesty. It involves a vulnerability to being misunderstood or taken for granted. At times only good humour and the ability to laugh at ourselves will oil the wheels that keep the love flowing. Open and vulnerable love means that we cannot hide behind religiosity or pseudospirituality and need to be willing to be seen for what we are.

Cultivating respect for one another will mean that we value and appreciate every individual for their human worth, never as converts or pew-fillers. The practise of honouring one another and promoting one another above our own self-interest will destroy the competitive instinct that is so destructive to mutual respect and dignity.

Finally, growing in understanding of one

another with all our idiosyncrasies, diversity of personality, and past history, will take time. Meaningful church takes time to grow, it has to be built carefully on the solid foundation of Jesus' life (1 Cor. 3:11). Jesus Himself is committed by His own words to build those powerful relationships. Unless He builds the house we labour in vain.

1.   Marshall, Tom, op. cit., p. 133.

RADICAL EVANGELISM

A New Look at an Old Commission

Pete Gilbert

This Pioneer *Perspective* gives the biblical basis for the theology of evangelism resting on the contention that God wants to communicate to His people of all time, all of the time.

Pete Gilbert reiterates the words of Paul to Colossae and clearly explains the role of the 20th century church and its people to 'proclaim the mystery of Christ' with clarity, wisdom and grace.

Therefore the role of the evangelist, as pointed out by this *Perspective* and Paul's words, is to pass on the good news and to equip and train others to do likewise.

The author writes that in the sphere of radical evangelism, plans need to be created and implemented. Pete Gilbert suggests a 5-point strategy that includes commitment, development, research, action and persistence, which are all fully explained in turn, and a handy help to any church wanting to grow in this decade of evangelism.

Catalogue Number YB 9728   £3.99

PROPHECY IN THE CHURCH

Martin Scott

At key times prophecy can shape your life. It is a gift which can radically change the course of a person's life or even that of a nation. Helping, inspiring and blessing, the individual is touched by words from the very Father heart of God, spoken to you as an individual or to the church as the body of Christ.

This book in the Pioneer *Perspectives* series is primarily concerned with the gift of prophecy and also the role and ministry of the prophet, leading one to ask:

Does this affect me? Can the Holy Spirit really dwell within me? Should I be expectant and desire change and challenge?

Martin Scott clearly states the Holy Spirit does reside in the Christian and He can manifest Himself through you at the right time in a variety of situations. Prophecy happens because God is a person who speaks. It is simply one of the things that the Holy Spirit does when He is free to do as He wishes.

This book is a sound study aid as we learn to be aware of and expectant for the Holy Spirit. Prophecy is a gift which we should expect to be poured out liberally during the age of the Holy Spirit. So much so, that Paul expected us to 'eagerly desire spiritual gifts, especially the gift of prophecy' *(1 Cor. 14:1)*.

Catalogue Number YB 9726   £3.99

THE ROLE AND MINISTRY OF WOMEN

Martin Scott

This two-part study in the Pioneer *Perspectives* series is the result of faithful research into an emotive subject; the role of women in the church—specifically in relation to their ministry as leaders. In a topic of heated debate the author has related the role women should play in the light of the revelation of God found within His Word.

The author points out that the Gospel comes to liberate regardless of differing perspectives; it makes us into the men and women God wants us to be. In Christ there is full and equal redemption for all people regardless of race, gender or social background *(Gal. 3:28)*.

So, how can women best be freed to serve effectively as God wants? If there are questions which remain, let us deal with each other graciously, knowing that God is always willing to shed more light where we are seeking answers, which will help us continue to walk in integrity before Him.

Catalogue Number YB 9725

£3.99

FOR YOUR NOTES